TAKE THIS JOB AND LOVE IT

Start living the life of your dreams with just a paycheck

Mildred Dillon, CPA

Financial Literacy House
650 Poydras St.
New Orleans, LA 70130
info@YourMoneyDr. com
www. YourMoneyDr. com

978-0-9884615-1-2 -- Take This job and Love It (ebook)
978-0-9884615-2-9 – Take this Job and Love It

Limits of Liability and Disclaimer of Warranty

The author and publisher shall not be liable for your use or misuse of this material. This book is strictly for informational and educational purposes.

RS CIRCULAR 230 DISCLOSURE: To insure compliance with Treasury Regulations (31 CFR Part 10, Section 10. 35), we are required to inform you that any tax advice contained in this correspondence including any attachments, was not intended or written by us to be used, and cannot be used by you or anyone else, for the purpose of avoiding penalties imposed by the Internal Revenue Code or other law or for the purpose of marketing or recommending to any other party any transaction, arrangement or other matter. If you desire a formal opinion on a particular tax matter for the purpose of avoiding the imposition of any penalties, our firm must be engaged for that purpose and we will discuss further the Treasury requirements that must be met and whether it is possible to meet those requirements under the circumstances, as well as the anticipated time and fees involved.

Warning – Disclaimer

The purpose of this book is to educate and entertain. The author and/or publisher do not guarantee that anyone following these techniques, suggestions, tips, ideas, or strategies will become successful. The author and/or publisher shall have neither liability nor responsibility to anyone with respect to any loss or damage caused, or alleged to be caused, directly or indirectly by the information contained in this book.

You and Your Job

I'm excited to publish this book, because most of my career, I've worked with or spoken to groups of entrepreneurs who take the risks of launching out on their own. To put it bluntly, they gamble each and every day, hoping they get clients and hoping their clients pay them or pay them on time. Some of them win, but as small business failure statistics show, many do not.

By picking up this book, you've made a different choice.

When I say, "take this job and love it." It's kind of a "no-brainer" that I mean be grateful that you have a job. Especially given the economic state of this country and in the world, many people wish they were working and had means to support their desired lifestyles. So that's a given. Appreciate the blessing!

By the way, gratefulness for where you are now and what you have now, no matter how little, is always the doorway to a higher level. I speak from experience. It took a lot of soul-searching and digging down deep when I went through painful times in my life. Now I know that step one of the way out is first of all to STOP and breathe. Then think, "What do I have to be grateful for?" So let's start right now being thankful for your employment, but here's another mental shift I'd like to introduce.

Even if you hate your job, are working in some very trying conditions, and even if you're not being recognized and not being appreciated, that job—for all its faults--is providing you "seed money." This seed money can get you to the next level if you use it properly.

This book is about what you can do to maximize every dollar that comes through your hands in the meantime. Here's why you have to: when you work a job, you're following someone else's rules. You're being told what to do. Your time is being controlled by someone else or by another person or a company. The IRS even goes so far as to define an *employee* as someone whose time you control. It's a key factor in determining if someone is an employee versus an independent contractor.

It's a very serious situation when you work a job because you're exchanging your life and time—which you can't get back—for money. I'm exchanging my time for money also, but the difference is I get to control my time. Now, I'm also taking a lot of risks to be in control, and I have no guarantees about the outcomes, but that's why there are advantages to having a job. Here are some:

1. You don't have to be creative. Someone else has done the thinking for you.
2. You show up, you do your job.
3. You get paid. Cha-ching!

Hopefully, you excel, get promotions and rewards, but that's an ideal situation. Even if you're not, you'll still be paid for the time, and that's why a job is my favorite type of income to work with: a check is on the way (almost) guaranteed.

Now of course, there's no such thing as a "guaranteed" job these days. I wrote this book to teach you to maximize the income from your regular checks. Whether it's every week or twice a month or however it works, you're going to get paid. Knowing that, we can have a plan for that money versus small business owners, who have to figure it all out and hope they get paid.

Are you getting the picture? Do you see what a goldmine you hold in your hands each payday? It's not how much you make. It's how much you keep. With a job, what you make—your income—is on autopilot. You just need to keep going for it to work. That's why I need you to take your job and love it.

This book offers tips and strategies on how to take that money and maximize it. Don't worry. It won't matter if you've blown every paycheck up until this point. Where do they teach money management? That's why I'm here and my goal is to lay a new foundation that gets you thinking and looking at your job and paycheck in a whole new way. With consistent money to manage, if you are a person who is teachable and will implement what you learn, you can really make fast progress.

What You Can Look Forward To

In this book, I'm going to show you my five-step M.O.N.E.Y system that can be used to take your finances to the next level. You'll probably raise your credit scores at the same time because how you manage YOUR money is how you'll manage other people's money. The two go hand-in-hand. These are the five areas I focus on while coaching clients and although we will not be able to go into extreme detail through this one book, it will give you enough to get you headed in the right direction.

The MONEY system includes:

- **M** - Multiply What You Bring Home
- **O** - Open and Pay the Bill Called "You"
- **N** - New Attitude towards Spending
- **E** - Exercise Your Right to Pay Less Tax
- **Y** - YourMoneyDr.com is your 24-hour Resource

Let's get started!

Step 1: Multiply What You Bring Home

There's a misconception that if you're struggling financially the best way to get out of that situation is to go out and get a part-time job or get overtime at your current job.

In some cases, that could work; but for the most part, that's not true. It's not how much you make, it's how *much you keep* that matters.

Stretching yourself even more and spending less time on you and with your family won't make things better.

For many who do bring home the extra check, it doesn't have much long-term impact due to the additional taxes and other lifestyle changes required to make that extra money (more babysitting expense, eating out more, etc).

When I sit down and I talk with someone about their finances, I come from a place of looking at what you have now, starting with the paycheck. As a CPA, there are some strategies I use to actually "multiply" the paycheck so the client takes home more the next paycheck or at least the paycheck after that. Grab pen and paper and start the process now.

Step 1 is to look at the actual paycheck stub. Now that right there is going to be a miracle for so many people because we've gotten away from the paper. We've gotten away from even looking at what we're making. But, step one is to get back to the basics, and it starts with looking at the numbers and what's coming out of your paycheck.

I cover taxes in a later section, but let's look at the non-tax deductions first and the biggest two are INSURANCE and RETIREMENT.

Consider this. If you rarely go to the doctor (which is not always a good thing), but you're paying top dollar for insurance, that's not a good use of your money. Anything you're paying for and not using is waste. But how do you know if it's top dollar? Do the math.

The deduction amount x the # of paychecks per year = annual premium

Here are the key questions:

- Is that cost for your entire family or just you as the employee?
- Does your plan option include doctor visit co-pays? If so, you're paying top-dollar.
- Does your plan option have a zero or very low deductible? If so, you're paying more than top dollar.

What you want to do is restructure your insurance costs to match your lifestyle. Now, if you're someone who sees doctors often, your group plan could be the best option out there. We have insurance specialists in our network who help you find out.

Other questions to ask are:

- 401K deductions - are you making money or losing money based on the last statement?
- Should you be in a different plan from the rest of the group due to your age?
- Should you be investing at all at this point?

If you're in debt, missing payments on bills or paying late because you're strapped for cash, or have no savings, then you need to put the investing on halt and address first things first. Timing can mean everything. This paycheck scan is just one of six different "scans" designed to find areas of waste or where you can cut costs. On average, we find $300 to $500 of extra pay, extra income each month.

Here's Your Prescription to Start Multiplying What You Bring Home:

Take a lookat your paycheck stub before moving on to the next step. If it was e-mailed to you, go get it from your inbox. If it was something where you had to log into your payroll system and download it, let's do that. The goal is to have a piece of paper in front of you so we can analyze your paycheck and determine what non-tax items are coming out each paycheck.

Visit www.YourMoneyDr.com for a free checkup. This is where we start the discussion with our clients and we encourage you to contact us at 866-2Doctor (236-2867) so you can input and send your numbers to us electronically. We'll send you back a customized Rx on what changes you should make with human resources officer at work in order to get more money in future checks.

Step 2: Open and Pay the Bill Called "You" (Save)

Before you see the actual increase in your paycheck, we need to cover an important step. We need to have a plan for why we want that extra money in the first place.

If you see more money, without a plan, the temptation will be to spend it, and the pay "raise" you just gave yourself will disappear.

With that, I want to challenge you to do some brainstorming and thinking about what it is you want your money to accomplish for you this year. Most people don't save because they feel they don't have enough "left over" to save. If this describes you, it's because you're actually planning backwards and putting yourself last on the list to be paid.

Remember the point I made earlier about you being controlled each day and exchanging your life and time for money - time away from your family that you can't ever get back? Doesn't it make sense to reward yourself for such a sacrifice and awesome commitment? Of course it does. I'll show you a few simple ways to start.

1. Save From a Plan

We've all heard the saying that "people don't plan to fail, they fail to plan". Master savers are master planners, and if you're going to pay yourself on a consistent basis, you have to plan for it. Saving starts with saving from a plan that clarifies your goals for why you're saving. Having a written plan means you'll always have your goal in view.

2. Start small.

It doesn't have to be a fortune starting out.

As the Money Doctor®, my focus is getting you into the mindset of saving, more so than the amount to save. When you begin saving and seeing your account grow, it's addicting and you'll want to save even more. It's like the best competition you've ever had, because you're competing with yourself, and you can't lose here!

Here, too, is the misconception, that plans have to be produced in fancy spreadsheets, software programs, or bound documents. Not so! It could even be a sheet of paper. Stories have been told of multi-million dollar ideas first being written on napkins. The key is to have it visible to you and a reminder at all times to keep you focused and on track. Here's a bonus tip. Writing it down has power, and science has proven that writing produces a special physiological connection from the hand to the brain, and you accomplish even more, faster.

3. Make Saving Automatic

I call this step the bill called "You" because that's what you're doing. Paying yourself. We just need to pay you first!

So the quickest way I began saving years ago, was to put saving on auto-pilot, by creating several of my savings accounts as actual "bill payees" in my online banking. Then I set up payments to flow from my checking into each of these accounts at regular times during the month. That way I didn't even see it in my checking account, but whenever the savings statements arrived, it was a great feeling to see all that extra cash accumulating. It's addicting!

And for those of you just starting out with saving, I prefer this method over the 401K, which operates in similar fashion with the money being taken before you see it. In this way, you have control over that money, and if an emergency arises you have access to it, without delay and without penalties.

Here's Your Prescription to Start Paying Yourself First:

I want to invite you to determine and write down an amount you can save in 30 days. This amount can be as little as $5 but commit to save something in the next 30 days.

THE MONEY DOCTOR®

Mildred Dillon CPA

866-2DOCTOR • cs@yourmoneydr.com

www.YourMoneyDr.com

Name: ____________ Phone: ________ Date: ________

℞

Next Appt: ____________

Write the amount you will commit to save for yourself here: ____________

If you bank online, create a bill payment that is sent to your savings account in frequencies that make sense. This will prove to you that you can save. Make a commitment to start now or with your next paycheck.

What other goals can you set and accomplish in 30 days? Open a savings account? Pay off a debt? Run your credit reports? Make a commitment by writing them down and keeping them visible so you can start to focus on them.

Step 3: New Attitude towards Spending

Financial advisors are looking at long-term planning and the "big picture" and that's always necessary for success. But when people are blowing through their money, living check-to-check and not doing the basics, they need a closer view of "today. "

What makes the Money Doctor® systems unique and effective is that they are designed to provide you snapshots of where your money is going now and help you set 30-day, 60-day, and 90-day goals to form new habits. But there's a reason why I'm so passionate about the details.

I live on the Gulf Coast and am blessed to say that I have survived some really tough challenges in our region: hurricanes Katrina and Rita (and others afterwards), the BP Oil Spill, credit crunch, and challenges in my own personal life that caused my income to take a tremendous nose-dive. Add to it the extra expense publishing books. I was forced to do things differently if my business and I would survive.

Even in the middle of the chaos, a strong vision and written plan kept me focused and on target. Within just four years since that time, I've published nine books and created two financial literacy programs to teach others how to rebuild their finances and make it on less. To date, three grants have paid me to teach both adults and young people. How did I survive? Spending cash. And it's a habit that's stuck with me.

Where's your money going?

Overall, spending cash helped me to eliminate the non-necessities like always picking up the tab at restaurants and coffee shops. When things got tight, I even used cash for business expenses (keeping receipts of course). Picture this, me walking into a gas station every single day of one week with a $20 bill in hand and out of my envelope system. That extra time and effort really got me paying attention to all the "business" meetings that weren't turning into real business or a bank deposit. I cut those trips down to just two days a week and worked in certain areas of the city instead of zig-zagging and that change alone created an extra $200 my first month.

We all know what we struggle with, and if you're overspending and not saving, I'm going to recommend you spend cash. Yes, even for your business, BUT (big but here) you need to spend cash with a system to keep up with the receipts and that's my version of the cash envelope system.

Statistics Show: Spend Cash, Spend Less

There are numerous cash envelope systems out there. I think mine is easiest to adapt to because it's not about having multiple envelopes to keep track of or writing down everything you do. My version replaces your debit card with a cash envelope. Simple. So where you would use the debit card, spend out of the cash envelope instead. Make sure and always replace the cash with a receipt and you'll have all the records you need for taxes. Start with a new envelope each week.

Where I wasn't a fan of cash before, I am now. My system works for all kinds of businesses I work with who primarily collect and spend cash. But now you have the system in place for the records. It made me an instant saver and when business got really good, I was still hardly spending which helped me save close to $20,000 in just 18 months! I have short videos at www.YourMoneyDr.com to help you get started. Here's your prescription to start spending less:

If you didn't do so, I want to invite you to watch the videos at www.YourMoneyDr.com and try the cash envelope system for yourself and your family. The goal is to use cash instead of the debit card.

Here's your prescription to start spending less:

If you didn't do so, I want to invite you to watch the YouTube video and try the cash envelope system for yourself and your family. The goal is to use cash instead of the debit card.

THE MONEY DOCTOR®
Mildred Dillon CPA
866-2DOCTOR • cs@yourmoneydr.com
www.YourMoneyDr.com

Name: ____________ Phone: ________ Date: ________

℞

Next Appt:

Step 4: Exercise Your Tax Rights to Pay Less Tax

Each January, many of the working class can't wait to file taxes so they can get a refund. Do you know what they need to be thinking about? Tax planning for next year's taxes.

You don't have to be wealthy and in the top 1% of income earners to need tax planning. Studies show that without it, you'll work through mid-May this year just to pay your tax bill for next year! Ouch! That's half of your working life to pay taxes, and not at all the way to build wealth or have the money from your job work for you.

Remember all the talk about how Warren Buffet's secretary paid more in taxes than he did one year? Typically, if you're an employee, and do nothing but show up for work, you're going to pay more in taxes than a business owner who takes home close to the same income because the tax deductions for you won't be obvious to most tax preparers. If they just enter the forms you give them and press the print button, I can tell you, you're paying too much tax. That's money that could be going into savings, set aside for a down payment, used to pay off student loans, or prepare for future tuition. It's YOUR money and time to exercise your rights to keep more of it!

You Probably Don't Need a Part Time Job. Just Pay Less in Taxes

As a CPA who prepares taxes for a living, I can look at your tax return and it will tell me all about your financial life. Based on what schedules you're using, and deductions you're (not) taking, and it will give me a pretty accurate picture of your financial activities. Because we've gone so electronic, few people even look at their returns each year or get copies. Truth is, the tax laws don't have to hurt. They can work for you or against you, it just depends on what side of the tax code you're on--and who's doing your taxes.

So. . . how much did you pay in taxes last year?

Just because you received a refund, doesn't mean you didn't pay tax

I want to share two real stories that illustrate my point.

Meet Client A who earned $125,000 per year as an employee and met with me to review his financial picture. After reviewing his returns from the prior year, he received a $9,000 refund on his tax return. But guess how much he paid in taxes? $40,000! He didn't even know it. Guess how much he owed in student loans? $40,000! He could have almost paid them off in a year with better tax planning on the front end.

Meet Client B who earned $36,000 per year with the school system, but also made an extra $2,000 per month with a lawncare business on the side, but was not reporting that income on his taxes or deducting expenses. He also received on average a $3,000 return each year, but the previous year his refund was lower because he paid $1,000 in taxes. Not only would the business deductions have helped him get that extra $1,000 back in his refund, but the extra business income would have helped him get the home loan he was trying to qualify for but was turned down because of "insufficient income to meet the debt. "

Get the picture? Both got refunds, but had no idea they really paid taxes.

Get a system to keep track of expenses all year

When you talk about keeping track of money, the most effective systems help you manage the paper and have what you need for tax time, but an effective system also give you those eye-opening totals of what you're spending so you can make changes before tax time.

Use Paper or Computers?

There's really no "right" way to keep track of your money, but you do need a system that fits your lifestyle and that you will feel comfortable with on an ongoing basis so you can keep it current. Apps are okay if you stay on top of the app and combine the totals from the app with your other financial totals. I find people just don't complete the process with an app and generally aren't getting in touch with their numbers.

The cash envelope system I introduced in the last chapter is my absolute favorite accounting system for barbers, stylists, landscapers, and other self-employed people who primarily handle cash. But remember, if you're spending your money on job expenses and don't get reimbursed for them by your employer, those are tax deductions that can help you pay less tax, and get a larger refund. You can keep the receipts in an envelope as well.

For people who prefer writing in notebooks or on paper, my pocket planner system is an inexpensive way to connect all the pieces of your financial life: monthly bills, debts, insurance costs, even business and work expenses or mileage. The worksheets start with the mail and get updated each week as you're opening your mail. That's the system--weekly, so it doesn't pile up and get overwhelming.

For most businesses I run across, I recommend QuickBooks. Not only does it pull the transactions into the program right from your bank account, so you never miss a tax deduction, but they offer a free 30-day trial as well to try it out.

So far, I've shared with you three systems: the cash envelope system, my pocket planner, and for business owners who are comfortable using technology, QuickBooks. Using any of those ways, you will stay on top of your numbers all year long and have the records you need for tax time to maximize your deductions and multiply your income.

Here's your prescription to start exercising your rights to payless tax

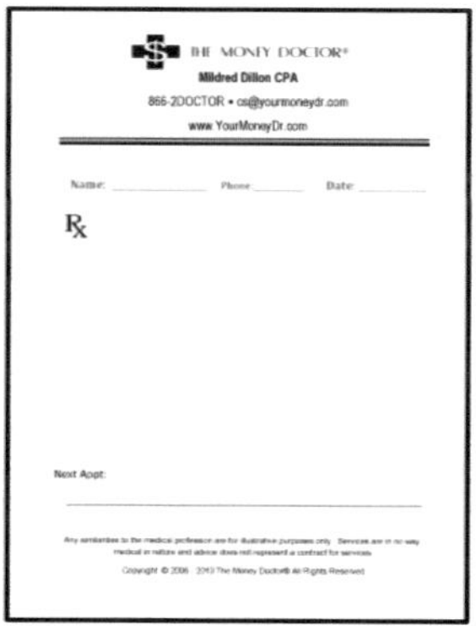

For this week's exercise, I want to challenge you to get that tax return and look at it and find the line that says, "Total tax." That is going to be key to giving you the picture of "Wow! I am paying tax. I need to look at are there some tax deductions that I can be taking so that we can have a different tax outcome for next year. "

Remember, by working through these simple steps you will not only impact your taxes come January of next year, but these steps also allow for that small money tree illustrated in step one to grow into that money oak tree—solid and dependable—in time. These steps help you dig in and grow financial roots that will allow you to take that job and its payroll check to grow and multiply YOUR money.

Step 5: YourMoneyDr.com

This book is a guide for you to begin taking steps to take your job and love it.

You've seen the various prescriptions that connect to special actions for those going through my coaching program. If you hadn't reached out to us, I hope that you will. Why? Because here's where we talk about some of the issues that could really be holding you back. As I said in the introduction, some problems are serious.

Hopefully, you see all the possibilities available to you from receiving a steady paycheck and managing that inflow. If you skipped any step and not taken action on the prescriptions I gave you at the end of each section, I recommend you go back and start them now.

I also invite you learn more about me and the system by visiting our website: www.YourMoneyDr.com. This is the hub for everything we offer that gives you an "Over the Counter" help with free downloads, a blog, and links to affiliate resources for you, your business, even your kids.

Even if you're not ready to take action yet, if you sign up for communications and updates in the newsletter, when you are ready, we'll be just a few clicks away.

Need Something Stronger?
"Over the Counter" Not Working?
Get a Checkup

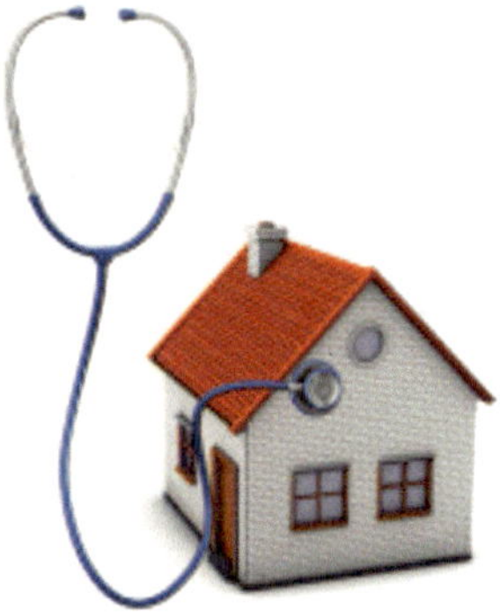

You may remember my personal story of struggle and how I turned things around in a very short period of time. I didn't do it alone. I had coaches in my life who taught me new skills, new ways of thinking, and literally pushed me to the next level in some cases. They didn't do it for free. I had to invest in me to get the help I didn't even know I needed. Now, I'm reaping the returns from that investment.

Maybe things aren't that serious, but you need accountability. You may even need a coach.

My team includes insurance, debt, credit, and legal specialists. We involve these specialists on your case as needed, but everything starts with a checkup at www.YourMoneyDr.com. Make it a great day, especially for your money, and I will see you soon.

Made in the USA
Monee, IL
05 November 2026

67377160R00024